Appliqué in Яeverse

Teri Henderson Tope

American Quilter's Society

P. O. Box 3290 • Paducah, KY 42002-3290

www.AmericanQuilter.com

Located in Paducah, Kentucky, the American Quilter's Society (AQS) is dedicated to promoting the accomplishments of today's quilters. Through its publications and events, AQS strives to honor today's quiltmakers and their work and to inspire future creativity and innovation in quiltmaking.

EXECUTIVE BOOK EDITOR: ANDI MILAM REYNOLDS
GRAPHIC DESIGN: ELAINE WILSON
COVER DESIGN: MICHAEL BUCKINGHAM
QUILT PHOTOGRAPHY: CHARLES R. LYNCH
HAND PHOTOGRAPHY: BOBBIE BROOKS
HOW-TO PHOTOGRAPHY: TERI HENDERSON TOPE

Additional copies of this book may be ordered from the American Quilter's Society, PO Box 3290, Paducah, KY 42002-3290, or online at www.AmericanQuilter.com.

Text © 2010, Author, Teri Henderson Tope
Artwork © 2010, American Quilter's Society

Library of Congress Cataloging-in-Publication Data

Tope, Teri Henderson.
    Appliqué in reverse / by Teri Henderson Tope.
        p. cm.
    ISBN 978-1-57432-657-4
    1. Appliqué--Patterns. 2. Quilting--Patterns. I. Title.
    TT779.T645 2010
    746.44'5041--dc22
                                                2009047400

American Quilter's Society
P. O. Box 3290 • Paducah, KY 42002-3290
www.AmericanQuilter.com

Dedication

To my treasures:

Dan and Jean Henderson, the most amazing parents a creative, messy child could ever want. You encouraged that part of me that saw the beauty in the sun flickering through leaves on a summer afternoon.

Mary Hammonds, my aunt, for letting me join her under that twig of a tree. You will forever be that angel on my shoulder.

Ginny Harris, my aunt, and the third of the Cape Hatteras trio (Mom, Mary, and Ginny). You shared your joy of quilting and the ocean—adventures and memories my daughters and I all enjoyed.

Andrea, Erin, and Hannah, my amazing daughters and my masterpieces.

Tim, my husband and partner in crime. You fill my life with love and laughter.

Liz Canty, JoAnne Purcel, Leslie Floyd, and Dorothy Adams— my living room quilting group, the S&M Quilters (that's "stitch and munch"). My mom always said, "You are who you hang out with." Thank you for encouraging me to go a little farther, reach a little higher, and okay, for also pulling me back when needed.

Introduction

Reverse appliqué is the process of cutting through background fabric to reveal the appliqué fabrics basted beneath.

Appliqué done in reverse creates a unique dimensional look and can be effective in many appliqué patterns.

The beauty of this appliqué process is in the fact that once basted, you are using large pieces of secured appliqué fabrics to create sometimes intricate designs—no more tiny, frustrating pieces.

The seam allowance in many cases is spread away from the appliqué instead of pushed under, creating smoother lines.

Imagine appliquéing a circle: Traditional appliqué would have you basting or pinning the appliqué in place, then sewing it down while pushing fabric (the turning or seam allowance) under the appliqué.

With reverse appliqué you draw the circle on the background fabric, baste the appliqué fabric beneath, and sew from the background using a thread color that matches the background. All of the turning allowance then fans out behind the background fabric and the drawn circle stays exactly where you want it. Works like magic every time.

LEFT: CONEFLOWER, detail. 30¼" x 29¾". Made by the author. Full quilt shown on page 74.

Reverse appliqué

Traditional appliqué

Tools of the Trade

Fabric

Having sewn on about everything imaginable, I do have my favorites. Choose the best fabric you can afford or get, and always, always prewash. I am not in favor of fabric surprises. If you spend all this time hand appliquéing your project, it is devastating to wash it and have colors migrate. Been there, done that, and don't want it to ever happen again!

Background fabric should be 100 percent cotton and have a thin, tight weave. Commercial hand dyes and batik fabric have a great hand and upon sewing, create crisp, turned edges. These fabrics may be harder on the sewing thread but result in great appliqué.

Thicker thread fabrics tend to fray and also create a bunchier seam line. When choosing a background fabric, look closely at the thread and its weave. Try to fray the cut edge; now imagine trying to appliqué a tiny little hole in it. Some fabric was made for reverse appliqué and some was not. Let's go with the ones that are; you'll thank me later.

As far as the appliqué fabrics are concerned, use whatever you like. This process has the appliqué fabric flat and basted to the back of your background fabric. Stick with 100 percent cotton, prewashed fabrics and you can't go wrong.

Thread

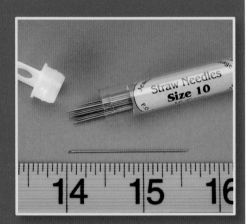

Needles

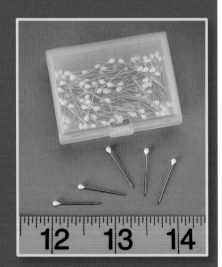

Appliqué pins

Thread

Again, I have used everything. My favorite is 50-weight cotton or silk when I can get it in the right color. Color is most important. Match your background fabric and thread color as closely as possible. This will make hiding that thread easier and the end result will knock your socks off.

Needles

I use straw/milliners #10 needles to appliqué. I use the needle as a turning tool and the extra length of this type of needle is my best friend in getting that seam allowance hidden. And yes, I also keep a needle-threader handy. Straw needles are notorious for their tiny eyes.

Appliqué Pins

Glass head ¾" appliqué pins are the perfect size for appliqué and especially for reverse appliqué. Their size keeps the thread from getting tangled without being too tiny to handle easily. The glass heads can be ironed without worry that they will melt and mark your fabric.

Light Box

I cannot live without this tool. I mark my blocks with it and also check appliqué fabric placement.

Fabric Markers

I use archival quality gel pens to mark appliqué patterns on my background fabric. Standard ink pens have a type of acid in them that helps to dry the ink. Archival ink does not have this agent added to it and therefore will not damage your fabric. These pens come in every color imaginable. I like to choose a color that matches the appliqué I am revealing, such as green for a green leaf, just in case a bit of my drawn line might show. The gel pens are permanent and their colors do not migrate. Please buy the best quality pen you can find to get the best quality ink on your quilt.

Fabric markers

Scissors

I have a favorite pair of 4" large-hole embroidery scissors; I had one blade serrated. I collect appliqué scissors. I have them in all sizes and colors. The 4" scissors are my working pair; the large holes are just the right size for my hands and ease that dreaded finger fatigue I get with tiny scissors. The serration gives me grip and control enabling me to get into the tightest of spots. Attached to a scissors fob on my shirt collar, they are always within reach. (Of course, I am always grabbing my chest looking for them.)

Scissors

Iron and Ironing Board

The key to great appliqué is keeping it nice and flat. Pressing your fabric before, during, and after the appliquéing makes all the difference in the world. Keep those seams flat.

Keep your iron clean, and always remember, once you start appliquéing, press your project from the back. That way, anything remotely damaging that might be on your iron will then be on the back of your project. If it is on your iron it will show up on your fabric. Happens every time.

Appliqué Preparation

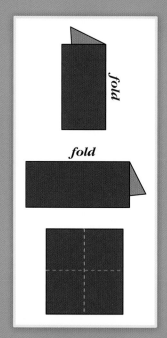

Figure 1

Photo 1

I know, I know… There is a lot of prep work in reverse appliqué. But look at the bright side—once you get all the preparations done, you get to sew! One color of thread, a sharp needle and a great pair of scissors… ahhhh, you are good to go.

Choose a background fabric, then wash, press, and cut it into blocks at least one inch larger than the required size. Fold the fabric block in quarters to find the center. Lightly press. (Figure 1)

After the appliqué is complete, you will measure and trim the block to the required size.

Using a light box, match the center of the block to the center marked on the appliqué pattern. Pin the pattern to the back of the background fabric. You can always move or remove the pins, so don't be stingy with them.

With the light box on, use a gel pen to carefully trace the pattern onto the right side of the background fabric. Gel pens are permanent, so lay off the coffee and use a steady hand. I also flick the light box on and off to check my progress and, okay, it entertains me. (Photo 1)

Remove the pins and pattern from the background fabric.

Using a pressing cloth to protect the ironing board, press the wrong side of the block with an iron to help set and dry the gel pen lines.

With embroidery scissors, make a small nip into all of the appliqué sections of the background fabric that will be reversed. This will make it easier to cut away the background fabric to reveal the appliqué after the fabrics are sandwiched. (Photo 2)

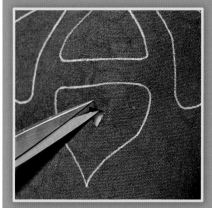

Photo 2

If your block contains more than one appliqué fabric, each fabric will be dealt with individually in this way.

There is no hierarchy or sewing order in reverse appliqué, so cut out a piece of appliqué fabric big enough to cover all the areas to be reversed in that color and press it with an iron.

Use a light box to double check that all the areas in the pattern are covered by the fabric piece. To do this, simply sandwich the layers right-sides up, lay them over the light box, and check that the entire pattern area is covered. Before you remove the block from the light box, use a few pins to attach the layers together. (Photo 3)

Photo 3

Thread a basting needle with colorfast thread and baste ½" around the outside of the appliqué design. The ½" measurement is important because in the reverse appliqué process you will be placing the turning allowance between the basting line and the pattern line. If you baste too close to the pattern line, you will not have enough room for this allowance. (Photo 4)

Pressing the basted fabrics with an iron helps mesh the appliqué fabric to the background fabric. Remember, the flatter the start, the flatter the result.

You are now ready to begin reverse appliqué. See? All that prep was worth it. You now get to actually sew!

Photo 4

How to Reverse Appliqué

The reverse appliqué stitch is the needle-turn appliqué stitch stitched on the background fabric instead of on the appliqué fabric. It's just opposite of the traditional needle-turn appliqué method—kind of like me.

Making the Perfect Quilter's Knot

Thread your appliqué needle with no more than 18" of thread. I know you hate to thread this needle and are tempted to use a longer thread, but doing so might put your eye out as you draw the needle towards your body. Just invest in a really good needle-threader. The shorter length of thread helps eliminate those dreaded knots and snags.

Knot the end with a quilter's knot. (Photos 1–7) To make this knot, lay the knot end of the thread horizontally on your index finger. Lay the threaded needle vertically across the thread and your index finger to make a T. Place your thumb over the intersection of thread and needle.

With your other hand, wrap the thread around the needle two times as you would to make a French knot. Without letting go of the thread, pull it gently under your thumb.

Now, keeping gentle pressure on the intersection of the thread and needle, with your other hand pull the needle away from your pinched thumb and index finger. Unpinch your thumb and index finger a little to allow the knot to slide along the thread. You should have a tiny knot. Snip off excess thread at the tail if necessary.

Photo 1

Photo 2

Photo 3

Photo 4

Photo 5

Photo 6

Photo 7

The Stitch

To start appliqueing, first cut away the background section to be appliquéd inside the appliqué line, leaving a scant ³⁄₁₆". Clip all the inside curves with 45-degree angle snips. Keep those scissors at a 45-degree angle as much as possible; this allows you something to turn under later. Large areas to be reversed should be cut in small sections one at a time. Cutting away excess fabric as you go—not in advance—will keep large areas flat and stable. (Photo 8)

Clip all inside/concave curves. You do not need to clip convex curves or straight lines. I tend to clip inside curves quite a bit, almost shredding the fabric but not quite. Clip up to and through the drawn line. The drawn line is part of your turning allowance.

Photo 8

Photo 9

Photo 10

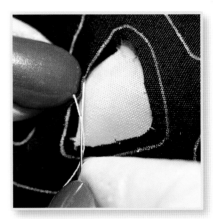

Photo 11

If you do not clip through the drawn line, you will see it on your background fabric after you appliqué, and remember, if you used a gel pen, it's permanent. (Photo 9)

With the needle coming from the backside of the background fabric between it and the appliqué fabric, hide the knot in the fold of the background fabric. (Photo 10)

With the needle, gently swipe the raw edge of the background fabric underneath the drawn line and between the background fabric and appliqué fabric. Finger press along this "swiped" area until you have a finger's length of fabric perfectly aligned and ready to sew. (Photo 11)

And yes, having my nails done does help to maneuver the fabric—at least that is what I tell my husband!

Photo 12

Pull the thread across the appliqué from the background at a 45-degree angle. Insert the needle just behind the exit point of the thread. The force of putting the needle through the fabric will automatically push the tip of the needle even with the exit point of the thread from the background fabric. Hence, you create a small straight tack as apposed to a diagonal tack. (Photo 12)

Bring the needle back up a few threads from the entry point, pull it tight and along the side of the fold. Nip the edge of the fold with the needle and pull the thread through the fabric. (Photo 13)

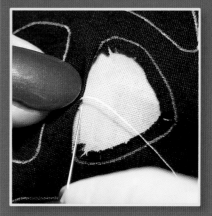
Photo 13

Continue to stitch using the needle to swipe the turning allowance under the background fabric, hiding the drawn line as you go.

To stop sewing, make a few stitches past the starting point. This will keep you from seeing a hard stop/start point on your appliqué. Pull the thread to the back of the appliqué fabric. Take a few tacking stitches through the appliqué fabric only and on the seam allowance side of the appliqué line. Bury the thread end under the appliqué. Cut off any excess thread. Ending thread in this way keeps everything nice and tidy on the back of your project—no loose threads to wiggle back under the appliqué and be seen on your finished quilt.

Press the completed appliqué from the back.

Those Dreaded Skinny Stems

To reverse appliqué skinny stems you first must realize that stems and reverse appliqué in general will turn out larger than the pattern that was traced. This is because the traced line is part of the turning allowance. Simply cut down the center of the stem pattern with appliqué scissors, a couple of inches at a time. Turn under and appliqué down one side of the stem and then up the other. With proper basting you should create smooth, even stems. (Photos 14 and 15)

Photo 14

Photo 15

Trimming Appliqué

It is very important to trim excess fabric from the appliqué on the back of the block. By doing so you reduce the bulk of the top, which eases the quilting process. Also, if a block requires more than one additional appliqué fabric, the excess fabric will get in the way, so it is best trimmed.

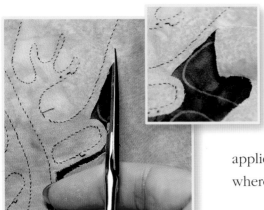

Photos 16a and b

Appliqué all areas that are the same color, then trim excess fabric. Lay the block flat, face down on a hard surface. Using appliqué or embroidery scissors, carefully trim off excess fabric a scant ¼" from the sewing line. Be very careful to check where you are cutting so as to not cut into the appliqué. It is not necessary to trim between every appliquéd area, as some areas are very close together. Trim only where you can leave a ³⁄₁₆" seam allowance. (Photos 16a and b)

Changing Appliqué Colors

Once you have finished sewing and trimming one appliqué color, baste and sew the next color using the same process you used with the first color. (Photo 17)

Floating Appliqué

Some of the designs in this book contain floating appliqué. These are appliqué pieces that float in the center of the appliqué pattern and do not directly connect to the background pieces. Floaters should be appliquéd first to the appliqué fabric. (Photo 18)

Photo 17

As these sometimes are very small pieces, it is not necessary to baste them individually. Use a ¾" appliqué pin to hold one edge down and ensure correct placement. Carefully cut away a small area at a time and sew a little bit at a time. Continue cutting and sewing until the whole floater has been appliquéd. (Photos 19a and b)

Photo 18

A few designs have appliqué within the appliqué, such as the centers of the morning glories. Treat these areas as you would in changing appliqué colors. Think floater within a floater. (Photo 20)

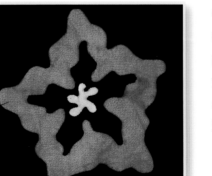

Photos 19a and b   **Photo 20**

Quilt: NOUVEAU GARDEN

NOUVEAU GARDEN, 65" x 75", made by the author

Finished size approximately 65" x 75"

The beautiful designs of the Art Nouveau period inspired this quilt. Amazing brilliant colors of commercially produced, hand-dyed fabrics jumped off the shelves and into my arms as I contemplated the quilt. It basically designed itself!

Creating the Quilt

Notes:

Prewash and press all fabrics.

You should have more than enough appliqué fabric following these cutting instructions. Scraps are always an option.

Background blocks and setting triangles are cut large for trimming later.

The appliquéd floral blocks should be trimmed to 13" x 13".

The Bumblebee frame should finish approximately 5" x 5".

Fabric Requirements

6 yards black background fabric

⅓ yard light brown for trellis border

⅓ yard dark brown for trellis border

Thirteen 15" squares or fat quarters of assorted hand dyes for flowers and flower block frames

6" square pink for bee frame

Scraps of yellow and gray for bee appliqué

Thirteen 14" squares or fat quarters of assorted greens for floral blocks, or you may do as I did in Nouveau Garden and use ½ yard cuts of four different greens

⅓ yard green for ivy

Cutting Instructions

Note: *See the Cutting, Trimming, and Layout diagram on page 20.*

From background fabric cut:

> One 57½" x 10½" rectangle for ivy appliqué block
>
> Thirteen 15" x 15" squares for floral appliqué blocks
>
> Sixteen 4½" x 4½" square blocks for trellis border
>
> Six 4" strips selvage to selvage for trellis border:
>
>> Two 18" long
>>
>> Six 7½" long
>>
>> Eight 15" long
>
> Five 19" squares for setting triangles:
>
>> Cut 4 in half (corner to corner) (Figure 2)
>>
>> Cut one crosswise into 4 corner pieces (Figure 3)
>>
>> Seven 1½" strips selvage to selvage for outer border
>>> (piece as necessary)
>>
>> Seven 2½" strips selvage to selvage for double-fold
>>> binding

From light brown cut:

> Nine 1" strips selvage to selvage

From dark brown cut:

> Nine 1" strips selvage to selvage

Figure 2

Figure 3

Quilt Center Construction

Note:

> *All seams are sewn with ¼" seam allowance. We will have no repeats of Teri's first quilt!*

Prepare and appliqué the 57½" x 10½" ivy header strip and the thirteen 15" x 15" floral blocks from the patterns on pages 24–53. Trim the ivy strip to 54" x 10½".

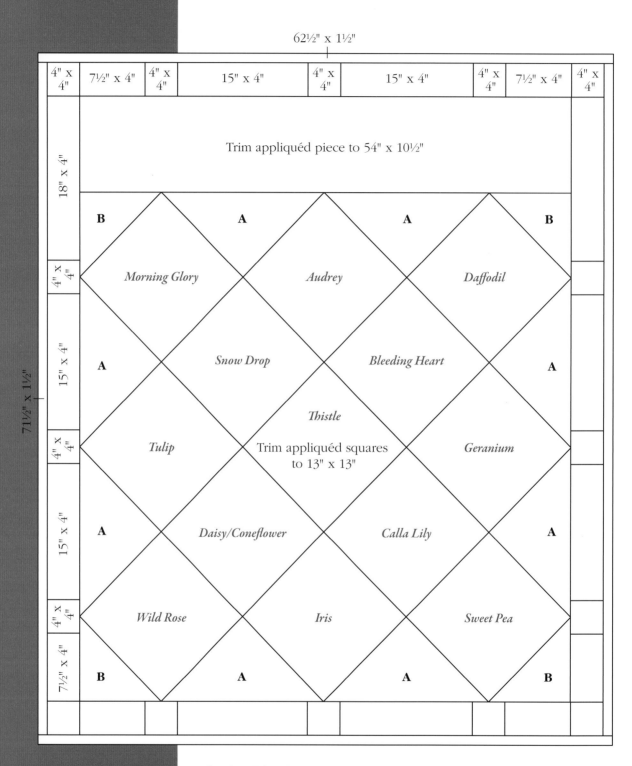

62½" x 1½"

| 4" x 4" | 7½" x 4" | 4" x 4" | 15" x 4" | 4" x 4" | 15" x 4" | 4" x 4" | 7½" x 4" | 4" x 4" |

Trim appliquéd piece to 54" x 10½"

18" x 4"

B   **A**   **A**   **B**

Morning Glory   *Audrey*   *Daffodil*

4" x 4"

Snow Drop   *Bleeding Heart*

15" x 4"

A   **A**

Thistle

Tulip   Trim appliquéd squares   *Geranium*
to 13" x 13"

4" x 4"

71½" x 1½"

Daisy/Coneflower   *Calla Lily*

15" x 4"

A   **A**

4" x 4"

Wild Rose   *Iris*   *Sweet Pea*

7½" x 4"

B   **A**   **A**   **B**

Cutting, Trimming, and Layout Diagram

A = Side Setting Triangles (need 8). Cut four 19" squares in half. Trim to fit (Approx. 18" x 12½" x 12½")

B = Corner Triangles (need 4). Cut one 19" square diagonally twice. Trim to fit (Approx. 13" x 9¼" x 9¼")

Start the appliqué for each block with whatever color floats your boat. Trim the completed floral blocks to 13" squares.

On a large flat surface or design wall, lay out the thirteen floral blocks in a pleasing manner. Place the corner and setting triangles on a surface as directed in the layout diagram. Sew the blocks and setting triangles together in diagonal strips. Press seams according to the arrows in the diagram. (Figure 4)

Sew the rows together, trimming the setting triangles as needed. Press the top.

Sew the appliquéd ivy rectangle to the top of the quilt. Press the seam toward the rectangle. (Figure 5)

Figure 4. Arrows indicate direction for seam to be pressed.

Figure 5

Trellis Border Construction

To create the trellis strips, sew one dark brown and one light brown strip to both long sides of each of the six 4" background strips. Press the seams to the background strips. Trim the strips according to the Cutting, Trimming, and Layout diagram on page 20—six 7½" strips, two 18" strips, and eight 15" strips. (Figure 6)

Figure 6

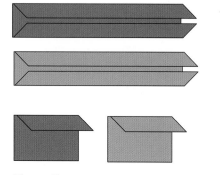

Figure 7

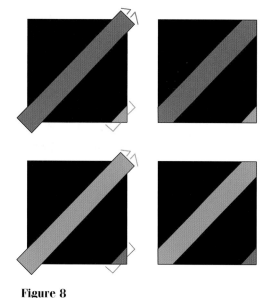

Figure 8

Figure 9

Make 4 corner squares with diagonal appliqué and twelve blocks with appliquéd crosses. To do this:

With an iron, press under ¼" on both long edges of the remaining light and dark brown strips. (Figure 7)

For the 4 corner blocks, appliqué 2 blocks with light brown appliqué in the center and dark brown at the corner, and 2 with the color placement reversed. Place the prepared strips across the 4½" background squares and appliqué into place in the center. Then appliqué the prepared alternate colored piece into the corner. Trim any excess fabric from the corners. (Figure 8)

For the twelve sashing blocks, the dark brown appliqué should be placed underneath the light brown appliqué to create a flow in the trellis design, so appliqué the dark brown prepared strips first to the twelve 4½" background squares corner to corner. Appliqué the light brown prepared strips crossways over the sewn dark brown strips. Trim any excess fabric from the corners. (Figure 9)

Lay out the quilt trellis border according to figure 10 on page 23. Pay close attention to the placement of the light and dark fabrics in the sashing and setting squares. Sew the squares and sashing rectangles together. Press to the sashing rectangles. As you sew the trellis borders together, match the appliqué and sew the light and dark brown strips so they look seamless.

Sew the side trellis borders to the quilt. Press the seams to the border.

Sew the top and bottom trellis borders to the quilt center.

Outer Border Construction

Measure down the center of the completed top. Piece together the 1½" outer border strips to this measurement. Sew to the sides of the quilt top and press to the outer border as shown in figure 10.

Measure across the center of the completed top, including the newly added side borders. Piece together the remaining 1½" outer border strips to this measurement. Sew to the top and bottom of the quilt top and press to the outer border.

Layer the quilt top, batting, and backing.

Quilt as desired (see page 71).

Add binding, label, and enjoy!

Figure 10

The Patterns

When my husband and I purchased our current home, it was clear that the previous owner loved to garden. With each season, new floral surprises greeted us as we walked out the door. Unfortunately, I am a quilter, not a gardener, and many of the lovely plants have disappeared due to lack of attention. This quilt, Nouveau Garden, pays tribute to that lost garden. Thank you, Shirley Washburn.

I have been told that a few of my designs are not horticulturally correct. No surprise! While some are easily recognizable, I have thrown in a few flowers that grow only in the garden of my mind. Therefore, you have my permission to do with them as you wish. I enjoyed prowling around the Internet finding these interesting tidbits, mostly from Wikipedia and Geocities. See what you can find (when you're not sewing).

Audrey

This design came about after a long day of doodling, something I am a bit famous for. Audrey is a purely imagined flower that resembles a certain outer space flower tended by Seymour Krelborn in the musical *Little Shop of Horrors*. My apologies if you now have the tune "Suddenly Seymour" stuck in your head.

Enlarge
pattern
200%

Bleeding Heart

We have all heard the term "bleeding heart." I truthfully was not thinking about liberals. I was picturing the genus *Dicentra* (and yes, I had to look that up). These flowers are usually pink, red, or white. They are so unique and delicate and have inspired many stories and folklore. I just could not have made this quilt and not included these beauties, which are also known as Venus's car, Dutchman's trousers, or lyre flower.

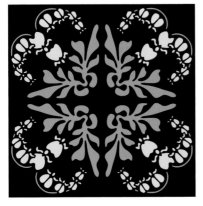 

Enlarge
pattern
200%

Teri Henderson Tope ❧ Appliqué in Reverse

Bumblebee

The humble bumblebee reminds us to embrace the honey of life and to make our lives productive while the sun shines. There can be no better way to be productive than to spend the day (rain or shine) quilting.

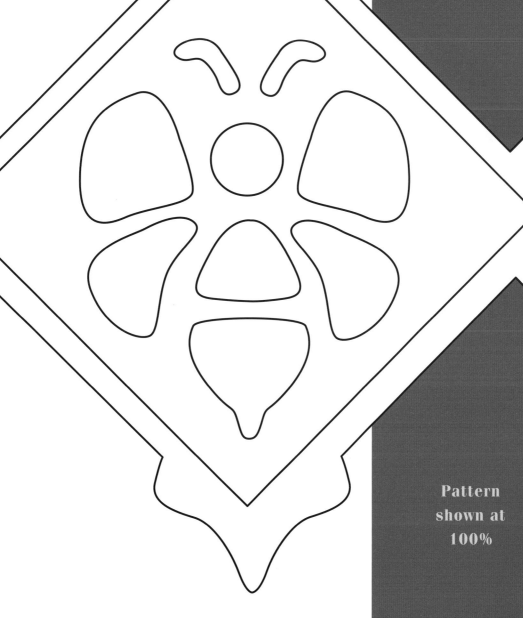

Pattern
shown at
100%

Calla Lily

The calla is a truly elegant flower. This plant is available in various colors—white, cream, yellow, gold, mango (which is a beautiful color— orangey gold), pink, and burgundy. As for the symbolism of this flower, the only meaning I found said it symbolizes ardor, which means feelings of great intensity and warmth, which is an entirely appropriate meaning for a flower on a quilt, don't you think?

Enlarge
pattern
200%

Daffodil

Daffodils are particularly interesting flowers and another of my favorites. Did you know that if you keep chickens, you might not want to bring daffodils into the house? A British old wives' tale says that if you bring daffodils inside when the hens are laying eggs, no chicks will be born alive. Kind of creepy! A lesser-known epithet when applied to military jargon is that to be called a daffodil is to be called a chicken. Whatever the story, chicken or egg, enjoy your daffodils.

Daisy/ Coneflower

I am a collector and avid reader of fairy tales and there is a wonderful story by Hans Christian Andersen called "The Daisy." My favorite quote from it comes from the daisy: "It [the daisy] thought, 'The sun shines upon me, and the forest kisses me. How rich I am!'" These little beauties are my favorite flowers and what I carried when I married my husband. Daisies are my preferred flowers to receive on special occasions. A simple color change and voilà! Coneflowers.

Enlarge
pattern
200%

Teri Henderson Tope ❧ Appliqué in Reverse

Geranium

Geraniums are grown in a variety of colors including white, red, pink, salmon, purple, magenta, and violet. Red geraniums have always been my favorite container plant, bringing back memories of the Fourth of July—Mom's front porch with flags flying and grape vine baskets full of geraniums hanging.

Enlarge
pattern
200%

Iris

Iris was a Greek messenger who used a rainbow as a path between heaven and earth. Ladies, this is the perfect flower to hit that fabric stash for! In the yard, mine grow in a small area just off my front walkway. It always amazes me that from such scary bumpy tubers the elegant irises grow.

**Enlarge
pattern
200%**

Ivy

My mother always sang this little ditty: "Mares eat oats and does eat oats and little lambs eat ivy. A kid'll eat ivy, too. Wouldn't you?" Well, I don't know what kind of diet she was on, but ivy is not included in my list of salad greens! Sewn into a quilt, ivy seems to make the perfect border. I kid you not!

Enlarge
pattern
200%

*reverse pattern for
opposite side*

Morning Glory

Poet Ella Wheeler Wilcox wrote, "A weed is but an unloved flower." So what's the story, morning glory? I remember morning glories growing wild along the fence in our back yard. Dad would pull them and cut them and drag out the weed killer, but to no avail. They always managed to return twofold.

Enlarge
pattern
200%

Snow Drop

"The Snow Drop" is another favorite story by Hans Christian Andersen from which comes the quote, "You are the first, you are the only one!" These white flowers bloom mostly in early spring but sometimes in mid to late winter, which makes them the earliest flowering bulb. This block was designed to be a bit asymmetrical to add a little life to your quilt.

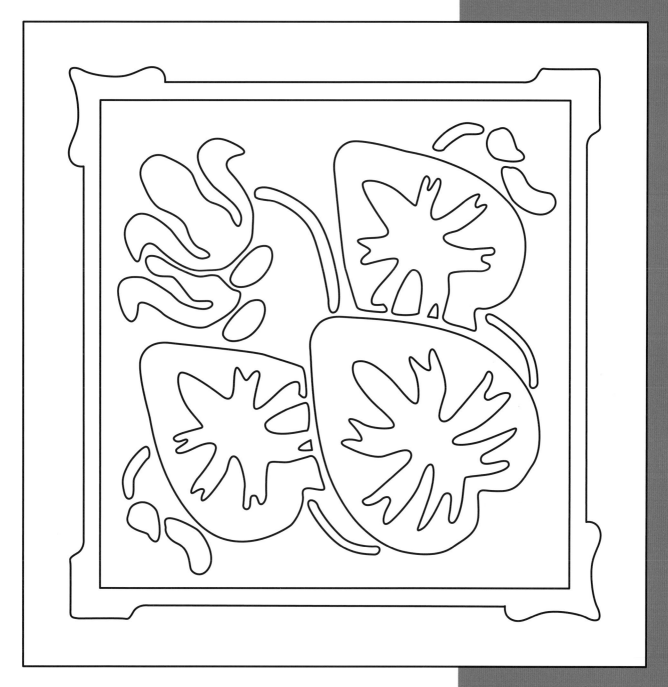

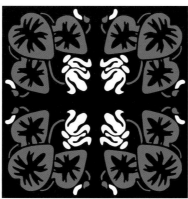

Enlarge
pattern
200%

Sweet Pea

The poet John Keats described the sweet peas with their "… taper fingers catching at all things, to bind them all about with tiny rings." The sweet pea blooms all summer and grows in an amazing array of colors. I took a little creative license and added a bit of vine to my design.

Enlarge
pattern
200%

Thistle

The story goes that the humble thistle is the national flower of Scotland because it saved the country from a Viking invasion. Apparently, the Norse invaders had planned a surprise attack at night, but while approaching a castle, one of the Vikings stepped on a thistle and cried out, alerting the castle to the attack and giving the soldiers time to put up a defense. I see a future quilt in this story don't you? I love the thistle for its wonderful design element and the much-needed speck of purple.

Enlarge
pattern
200%

Tulip

I have always associated the tulip with the Dutch. However, I was surprised to find out that the tulip is not a native Dutch flower, but came from the gardens of Constantinople; the Turks had been cultivating tulips from as early as 1000 AD, making this a truly old flower. My design gives homage to the wonderful row of tulips that treats my family in late spring.

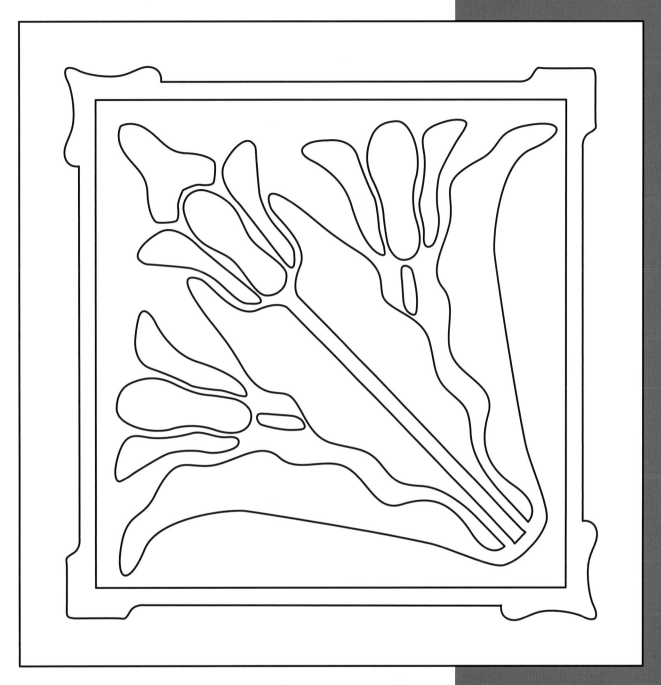

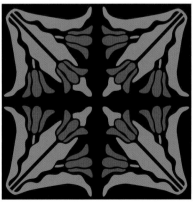

Enlarge
pattern
200%

Wild Rose

This was the first block I designed for my quilt. The rose is the flower goddess or spirit messenger for true love—a very romantic flower. Who doesn't admire the simple beauty of a rose? While quilting friends have said this block reminds them of poppies, I had roses in mind. This block is a tribute to Rosethel Thomas Tope, my wonderful mother-in-law. Whichever rose you prefer, as Shakespeare wrote, "That which we call a rose by any other name would smell as sweet."

Enlarge
pattern
200%

Wallhangings:
DOODLE IN REVERSE

DOODLE IN REVERSE, 28" x 28", made by the author

This little beauty followed me around for a long time. Once the appliqué fabrics were basted in, I was able to take it along with me. It has seen airport and hospital waiting rooms, traveled to quilt shows, and attended a retreat or two. Just a sharp needle, one spool of thread, and my handy dandy scissors and I was ready to go. Referred to as "that purple thing" by my quilting friends, I think I gave it a better-suited name, don't you?

Fabric Requirements

Note: Prewash and press all fabrics.

1 yard brown background fabric
½ yard lime green binding and appliqué
    fabric
Fat quarters for appliqué:
    purple
    orange
    white
    yellow
    green
    green print

Construct the Wallhanging

These appliqué fabrics could be gleaned from scraps in your fabric stash as mine were.

Prepare and reverse appliqué the design onto a 30" x 30" square of background fabric.

When the appliqué is complete and pressed, trim it into a 28" x 28" block.

Sandwich the completed appliqué block with batting and backing. Baste.

Quilt as desired. In this instance I simply ditch-stitched the appliqué and echo-quilted in ¼" increments around the whole design. Add binding.

Remember, this is a great take-along project and before you know it, you, too, will have a DOODLE IN REVERSE.

Enlarge
pattern
400%

STARTING BLOCK

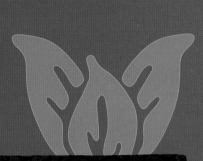

STARTING BLOCK, 17½" x 17½", made by the author

Finished size 17½" x 17½"

*T*designed this little quilt for a class sample. I had many people asking me to teach them reverse appliqué but they were not sure they wanted to commit to an entire quilt. This is a great class and first-reverse-appliqué project. I chose the daisy as my sample, but feel free to pick your favorite flower pattern and then coordinate the perfect fabrics for your very own one-block wonder.

Fabric Requirements

> 14" x 14" square of background fabric for appliqué
> 13½" x 13½" square of accent fabric cut into 4 triangles for border
> 13" x 13" square for leaves
> 13" x 13" square for flowers
> Scraps of yellow for flower centers
> 19" x 19" square of quilt batting
> 19" x 19" square fabric for backing
> ¼ yard fabric for binding

Construct the Wallhanging

Prepare and reverse appliqué your flower onto the background fabric. When the appliqué is complete and pressed, trim to a 12½" x 12½" block.

Cut the 13½" x 13½" square of accent fabric into 4 triangles. (Figure 1)

Sew these triangles to the 4 sides of the quilt block, pressing the seam to the triangle.

If necessary, square up the block to 17½" x 17½".

Layer and baste the quilt top, batting, and backing.

Quilt as desired. See "What Does 'Quilt as Desired' Really Mean?", page 71.

Add binding.

Voilà! A one-block wonder!

Use the Daisy/Coneflower pattern on page 35.

Figure 1

THREE BLOCKS

FINISHED SIZE APPROXIMATELY 17" x 50"

This cute little table runner was created to use a remnant of my favorite fabric. (I would love to see this color range in a whole quilt.) This is also my daughter Erin's favorite project in the book. One look at the completed runner and she declared, "Fierce! Can I have it?" Seeing that she was only 14 at the time, I took this as a compliment.

Fabric Requirements

½ yard background fabric for appliqué cut into three 14" x 14" blocks

½ yard accent fabric cut into 2 13½" x 13½" squares

¼ yard fabric for binding

⅔ yard fabric for backing

24" x 54" piece of batting

THREE BLOCKS, 17" x 50", made by the author

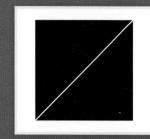

Figure 1

Construct the Table Runner

Prepare and reverse appliqué three flowers of your choice onto the three squares of background fabric. After the appliqué is finished and the block is pressed, trim these squares to 12½" x 12½".

Cut the two 13½" x 13½" squares of accent fabric diagonally to create four triangles (figure 1).

Lay out the quilt per diagram (figures 2 and 3).

Sew the triangles to the sides of the quilt blocks as indicated, pressing the seam to the triangle.

Sew the quilt blocks together to form the table runner.

If necessary, square up the sides of the table runner.

Layer and baste the quilt top, batting, and backing.

Quilt as desired. See "What Does 'Quilt as Desired' Really Mean?", page 71.

Add the binding.

Figure 2

Figure 3

Use the Audrey pattern on page 25.

Borders:
MORNING AT THE CABIN

MORNING AT THE CABIN, 95" x 95". Pieced by Liz Canty, appliquéd by Teri Henderson Tope, and quilted by Jane Williams

FINISHED SIZE APPROXIMATELY 95" x 95"

The borders of your quilt offer a perfect backdrop for reverse appliqué and add that extra bit of pizzazz to your quilt. How many of us have random quilt top UFOs (unfinished objects) tucked away just because they need that something extra? Ladies, get out those needles! It's time to reverse appliqué a border!

My best friend, Liz Canty, pieced this beautiful Log Cabin quilt, MORNING AT THE CABIN. I do not enjoy piecing (understatement), so this was the perfect joint project. I knew I wanted appliqué in just two of the corners of the border and left the other two corners up to the machine quilter (Jane Williams of Lady in Thread), making this truly a group quilt.

To replicate MORNING AT THE CABIN, make a center top of thirty-six 13" x 13" (unfinished size) Log Cabin blocks. To make a border like mine, follow these directions: (Yes, you have to use math!)

The appliqué was completed using scraps from the pieced quilt top.

Decide how wide your borders are going to be. In the case of MORNING AT THE CABIN, this measurement was 12".

The width of a piece of yard goods is approximately 44" (on a good day). Use 40" to account for manufacturing and shrinkage.

Divide the border width into 40. This yields the number of border cuts available from the width of fabric. Example: Three 12" wide borders can be cut from 40". A 4" width will be leftover and could be pieced for the fourth border if there is enough length to deal with.

To get the yardage needed for the length of the border, measure across the quilt in both directions. (Figure 1)

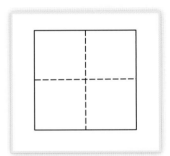

Figure 1

Figure out the longer of these two measurements and add double the border width if mitering. For example, for a 12" border, add 24" to the longest measurement (you're adding 12" for a miter on either end of your border strips).

Divide this longest measurement by 36 (the number of inches in a yard). Round this number up to the nearest yardage measurement, then purchase this amount of fabric.

Example: *The longest border on a quilt including the addition of mitered fabric is 76".*

Divide 76 by 36. 76 divided by 36 is 2 with a remainder of 4. You will need 2 yards and 4" of fabric. Round this up to the nearest yard measurement and purchase 2¼ yards of fabric for the borders. But wait! You can only get three 12" borders from 40" of fabric width. You can choose to piece the fourth border from the leftover cuts or buy additional yardage (4½ yards).

MORNING AT THE CABIN *12" Border Construction*

Notes:

The borders on this quilt were not mitered, but instructions are given here for doing so.

Measure the quilt top width and length through the center of the top, not along the edges.

Measure across the width of the quilt top and add 24". Cut two 12" strips this length.

Measure down the length of the quilt top and add 24". Cut two 12" strips this length.

In a large area, lay the borders out around the quilt center.

Mark the Borders

The appliquéd lattice in the corners extends into and connects or bridges with both border strips. To ensure the proper transition from one border strip to the other, follow these easy directions:

Decide where to place the appliqué. To keep from getting confused, pin a piece of paper to the area to be appliquéd with arrows indicating where the border attaches to the quilt and in which direction the appliqué is to go.

On the right side of the borders, draw a 45-degree angle with chalk across the corners. (Figure 2)

On a light box, trace the appliqué onto each border strip making sure to place the appliqué in the right direction on the strip. Start or stop drawing the appliqué at the 45-degree drawn chalk line.

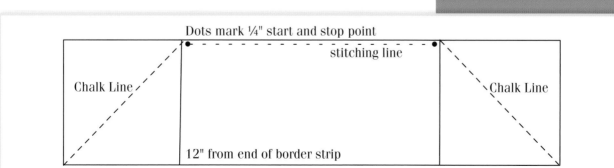

Figure 2

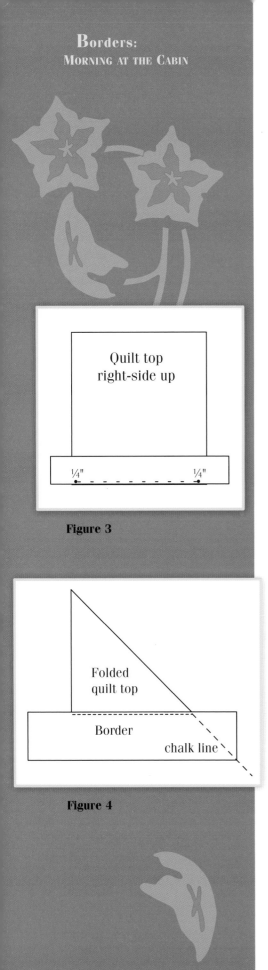

Figure 3

Figure 4

Appliqué the Borders

Do not appliqué areas that cross the corner chalk line. These will be appliquéd after the borders are sewn to the quilt.

Reverse appliqué the beautiful morning glories across the quilt borders.

Tip: If the large length of border fabric is too bulky and twisting as you go, fold or roll up the dangling end and secure it with pins.

Attach the Borders

You now should have four appliquéd borders with some unfinished appliqué at the corners. Place a border strip on a flat surface. Measure 12" from each end of the border and with a fabric marking tool, mark this measurement. (Figure 2, page 63)

Pin the border to the quilt top matching the 12" mark on the border to the corner of the quilt top.

With a ruler make a dot ¼" inside of the 12" mark on both ends of the border strip. (Figure 3)

To sew a mitered corner, lay the quilt top on a flat surface. Fold the quilt top diagonally so that adjacent borders line up. Lay a ruler along the border on the 45-degree angle. Line up the point where you started sewing the border strip to the quilt top with the 45-degree angle. (Figure 4)

Lightly draw a chalk line from the sewing point to the outer edge of the border. Remove the ruler and carefully pin. Sew on this marked line from the quilt top out.

Lay the quilt flat and check that the border is flat and sewn where you want it. Then, and only then, trim the seam to ¼" from the sewn line. Finger press the miter and border intersections flat. Then, with an iron, press all seams to the quilt top and press miters flat.

Repeat with the other three corners.

At this point, finish the corner appliqué.

Complete the quilt by layering, basting, quilting, and binding.

Morning Glory Border End

Enlarge
pattern
200%

Morning Glory Border Corner

Enlarge
pattern
200%

Morning Glory Border Filler

Enlarge
pattern
200%

Teri Henderson Tope ⚬ Appliqué in Reverse

Lettering: HOUSEWORK MAKES YOU UGLY

HOUSEWORK MAKES YOU UGLY, 24" x 18", made by the author

T The designer in me loves the process of adding words to quilts and using fonts that enhance the overall design.

24" x 18" FINISHED

When I print them out I can also take a marker to the letters, enlarging some of the thinner lines and making them more appliqué-friendly. I can move the letters or words apart to arrange them or play around with the spacing while they are in the computer.

Reverse appliqué and lettering fit together like perfect puzzle pieces. Imagine trying to appliqué even the simplest of fonts on a project. Traditional appliqué would have you pinning or basting these tiny pieces onto your background and turning under tiny seams. More often than not, those pieces move or distort.

With the reverse appliqué process, drawing the lettering onto the top of the background fabric keeps all the letters exactly where you want them. One large piece of appliqué fabric is basted to the back and nothing shifts or moves, offering incredible stability.

Why not add a little text to the front of your next quilt? The design possibilities of enhancing and embellishing a quilt with words are endless.

Tip: Always make a test block before actually marking on your quilt top. You want to ensure that you can successfully appliqué your chosen font before doing so on your quilt. You can always enlarge, reduce, add, or take away spacing to bring out the best result.

I don't know about you, but I have never seen a person look beautiful while cleaning a messy house! My kids think I get pretty ugly while cleaning ours.

Fabric Requirements

12" x 18" rectangle for appliqué background

Fat quarter for appliqué (The excess fabric should be saved and used in the strip-pieced border.)

Assorted red scraps of fabric strips pieced into a rectangle at least 15" x 27" (or ½ yard of accent fabric for border)

⅔ yard fabric for backing

20" x 26" piece of batting

¼ yard for binding

Ten ½" buttons

Construct the Quilt

Prepare and reverse appliqué the letters onto the background fabric.

Strip piece the border fabric by piecing randomly cut different sized fabric strips of assorted reds. These are then sewn together with ¼" seams and pressed flat. Slight angles lend an added design element. Just straighten up every couple of rows with a rotary cutter and ruler as you add strips.

**Enlarge
pattern
200%**

Measure across the width of the appliquéd block. Cut two 3½" strips this length from the strip-pieced border fabric. Sew to the top and bottom edges of the block.

Now measure across the length of the appliquéd block. Add 9" to this measurement. Cut two 3½" strip-pieced border fabric strips to this length. Sew to the sides of the block, mitering the corners as you go.

With all the seams involved in strip-piecing those borders, press the border seams to the center block.

Sandwich the quilt top, batting, and backing.

Quilt. See "What Does 'Quilt as Desired' Really Mean?", page 71.

Sew on buttons.

Add binding.

Hang this little masterpiece in a very noticeable place in your home. It is sure to make your guests smile and they will then cut you a little slack for any clutter they catch you with.

Housework Makes You Ugly!

What Does "Quilt as Desired" Really Mean?

While a lot of designers instruct you to "quilt as desired" so they don't have to get into crazy detail on how to quilt the quilt, I want to give you my insight and method into quilting my reverse appliqué creations.

Layering the Quilt

First, get your quilt top as flat as possible. If it is not flat when you start out it surely will not be flat when you are done. Press the quilt top from the back with a pressing cloth until nice and flat. Press the backing.

Find a surface large enough to tape down the entire quilt. Using painter's tape (I love it because it doesn't gum up your quilt or surface and it comes in a lot of great colors), securely tape the edges of the quilt backing right-side down. Make sure it is taut but not stretched or pulled.

Next lay out the batting smoothing it out with no wrinkles or folds. Make sure to remove any stray threads.

Top these layers with the nicely pressed quilt top right-side up. Closely examine the top to make sure no threads are showing under lighter areas of the quilt. Trim any seams that may cause shadowing.

Basting

There are two schools of basting: pin-baste or needle-baste. Here are my thoughts: If you are going to machine quilt, pin every 2 to 3 inches with safety pins made for quilt basting. You don't want a lesser quality pin rusting the quilt. If you are going to hand quilt, baste with needle and colorfast cotton thread every 2 to 3 inches.

Quilting

The Big Question to answer is, "Do I quilt it by hand or by machine?" I prefer to hand quilt my appliqué creations but sometimes that just isn't possible. Look at the amount of appliqué on the quilt. Then answer the following questions:

* Do you have a deadline?
* Will there be enough time to quilt this item?
* What will be its primary use? Is it to be used on the wall or bed?
* Who is the primary user?
* At which method do you excel?
* Are you faster and better at either option?

Always put forth your best work. As my mom always said, "It isn't worth doing if you are not going to *try* to do it right." I have a friend (Leslie Floyd) who loves to hand quilt and does it beautifully but struggles at machine quilting. By the way, she also primarily makes pieced quilts and

DOODLE IN REVERSE,
detail showing echo quilting.
Full quilt shown on page 54.

has hand quilted just about each one of them. So she would most likely choose to hand quilt her quilts. This is supposed to be fun! Do what makes you happy!

Quilting Designs

Another big dilemma is, "How do I quilt this?"

Lay out the quilt so you can see the entire top. I always start my quilting design by what I call structure quilting. These are the foundations of my quilting—areas that just scream to be quilted such as border and block ditches (seam lines). Structure quilting stabilizes the quilt so that you can then do intricate quilting in the open areas. It keeps straight lines straight and curved lines curved. Structure quilting also eases any distortion created by additional quilting.

I like to ditch-stitch each of the reverse appliqué motifs. This makes them just a bit more dimensional and also cleans up any slight imperfection with my appliqué. The saying, "It will quilt out," really works in this instance. The appliqué line will fold under just a tiny bit more creating a perfect edge to the appliqué. It's like magic.

For all other areas of the quilt I like to repeat the motifs of the appliqué such as a flower or leaf. These can easily be enlarged or reduced to fit in the area needed. All areas of the quilt should have similar amounts of quilting. If you are going to do intricate quilting in one place you should plan on doing it across the whole of the quilt.

I am also a big fan of echo quilting. Echo quilting is simply quilting ¼" away from the appliqué or pieced edge, in a sense echoing the appliqué.

If you have used fabric that has a very busy pattern you may want to quilt those areas with a simple or allover pattern. Your quilting stitches will get lost in the busy pattern. Busy patterned prints could also be outline quilted—simply quilt around the fabric's printed design.

Just remember, it's your quilt! If you want to quilt your name in it, do it. If you want bunnies hopping around the corners or butterflies floating around your flowers, just quilt them right in.

Quilt Gallery

I love the patterns in this book and a few from my company, Material Girl Designs, that contain reverse appliqué, not just because they inspired me to make the NOUVEAU GARDEN quilt, but because they lend themselves to so many adaptations.

Not being one of those quilters who ever likes to make the same quilt twice, I along with a few of my amazing friends have created a wonderful quilt show featuring reverse appliqué and the Nouveau Garden patterns. My goal in writing this book was to encourage creativity, so please take these patterns and give them your own personal touch. Enjoy the show!

Teri Tope's Home for Wayward Blocks

Having the habit of taking as many classes from as many teachers as possible, I have quite a collection of wayward blocks. You know, those little treasures that you are not sure what to do with but can't throw away—not exactly a UFO (unfinished object), just an orphan block waiting on the perfect project.

Well, wait no longer. Use those little works of art to embellish just about everything you own. Image a plain little pillowcase turned into the perfect gift with a beautiful reverse appliqué block (okay, you could also use those pieced things).

Blocks can be sewn to the back of a jacket or turned into the perfect pocket. Make all your

ROUND ROBIN QUILT, 35"x35", Naomi O'Harra

quilting friends jealous with the addition of a block to a simple handbag. Hey, you made it! Show it off!

Quilter Naomi O'Harra took one of my reverse appliqué classes and created a beautiful Coneflower block. Naomi is a member of the Goodtime Quilters Guild of Circleville, Ohio. In 2008, guild members exchanged blocks for a round robin. Naomi's group included seven quilters. Each quilter exchanged her block with another person in the group.

She then added a border to the block she received. Upon completion of that border, she passed the block on to another quilter. This rotation continued until each of the seven members had added a border to the original block.

Naomi chose to use her "wayward Coneflower block" as her original block in the exchange. Not only did she receive back a beautiful wall hanging, it also received an Honorable Mention in the guild's local show. Not bad for a little wayward block!

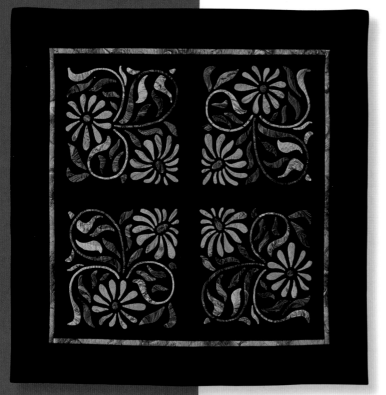

Coneflower, 30¼" x 29¾".
Made by the author.

Monarch Butterfly, 40" x 45". In this quilt the black fabric was used as the background. Wing fabrics were reverse appliquéd. The whole butterfly was then cut out of the black background fabric with a ¼" seam allowance, and then appliquéd to the background fabric. Designed and sewn by the author.

Wayward block, sewn by author. Added to the pocket of a Lazy Girl Designs bag.

Daffodils in the Garden, 108" x 108". Designed and sewn by the author.

Appliqué in Reverse ❧ Teri Henderson Tope

GREEN DRAGON, 20" x 30". Made by Janice Apel. Janice chose beautiful oriental inspired fabrics for her version of the Red Dragon pattern.

RED DRAGON, 20" x 30". A trip to Japan inspired this design by the author.

SUE'S FANTASY FLOWERS, 20½" x 20½". Designed and sewn by Naomi O'Harra for her daughter, Sue Schmelzer.

DIANA'S CALLA LILY, 18¼" x 18¼". Sewn by Naomi O'Harra for her daughter-in-law, Diana O'Harra.

FIRST KISS, 33" x 43". Designed by Arthur Rackham; sewn by the author.
I combined a couple of illustrations by Arthur Rackham to make this quilt,
altering them a bit to make them more appliqué friendly. The dark green
(almost black) fabric is the background fabric. The complete pattern was
drawn on one piece of this dark green fabric. I then reverse appliquéd the
other fabric appliqués.

RESPICE/PROSPICE, 30" x 30" working clock. Sewn for a 2000 millennium challenge by the author. Respice/Prospice means looking back /looking forward in Latin. I believe we do just that as quilters—one stitch at a time. The green leaves appliquéd behind the ruched flowers in the center of the quilt are reverse appliquéd, as are the numerals around the clock.

TWISTED POSIES, 13" x 14". Designed and sewn by Marilyn Reeves using NOUVEAU GARDEN patterns.

SUN AND SHADE, 61½" x 61½". Designed by Janice Apel using NOUVEAU GARDEN patterns. Quilted by Acorn Quilting.

Special Acknowledgments

HIBISCUS BLOOMS, 25" x 55". Designed and sewn by the author to commemorate her parents' trip to Hawaii. Teri's mother brought back some wonderful Hawaiian inspired fabric, none of which made it into the quilt.

RIGHT: Detail of Teri's first quilt

Acorn Quilting Co., Karen Weiler
Karen Weiler at **QuiltPox2@msn.com**

A Lady in Thread, Jane Williams
jane@aladyinthread.com

Lazy Girl Designs
www.lazygirldesigns.com

Material Girl Designs
www.materialgirldesigns.com

The Goodtime Quilters Guild
www.goodtimequilters.org

The Glass Thimble
www.glassthimble.com

We've Got the Notion
www.wevegotthenotion.com

Bobbie Brooks—hand photographer extraordinaire

Andi Reynolds—editor and author therapist

Elaine Wilson—graphics and forensic drawing specialist

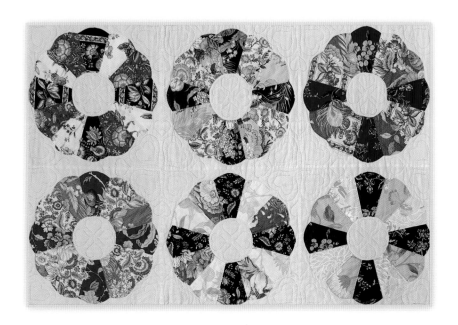

About the Author

Teri Henderson Tope has been a lifelong seamstress and a quilter since 1982. She was taught to sew by her mother, Jean Henderson, who was also her 4-H advisor. ("Joyful Jumper" was not very joyful; Teri must have resewn that zipper five times until it was perfect.) She did manage to learn how to sew correctly so that now she can break all those rules and invent a few of her own. Her first quilt had ⅝" seams. Need we say more?

Teri's quilting life really started with a pregnancy and six weeks of bed rest. Anyone who knows her knows that this would have been almost impossible for her to do were it not for an *American Patchwork and Quilting®* magazine and a box of chintz fabric samples. That first quilt was an appliquéd Dresden Plate quilted to a bed sheet (detail shown on opposite page).

And the rest, as they say, is history. Two more beautiful daughters and many more quilts were to follow, all culminating in this adventure titled *Appliqué in Reverse.*

Teri and her husband run Gumshoe Studio, a graphic design and web-based marketing firm out of their home in Worthington, Ohio. **www.gumshoestudio.com** She owns Material Girl Designs, a pattern business, **www.materialgirldesigns.com,** and is the partner of Liz Canty in their business, We've Got the Notion, **www.wevegotthenotion.com**

Teri is a member of the American Quilting Association, the National Quilting Association, the Quintessential Quilters, The Appliqué Society, the American Quilt Alliance, the Worthington International Friendship Association, and the S&M Quilters (that's "stitch and munch" quilters) along with a few other organizations because she has a problem with saying the word "no."

She has displayed quilts in many national and international quilt venues winning a ribbon or two. She also teaches and lectures and was given the honor of representing the city of Worthington by teaching quilting in its sister city, Sayama, Japan. Teri's passion for quilting is evident in her designs and she is most happy when she actually gets to sew. "Finishing a quilt is like saying goodbye to an old friend," she says.

Quilting has been Teri's joy. It has given her a voice and she hopes to share that with you in this book.

Life is too short, so enjoy it…quilt!

THE END QUILT, 17" x 26", designed and sewn by me! Could there be a more perfect ending for my book?!

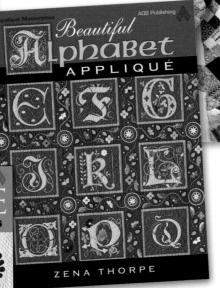